This Guest Book Belongs To

....

Welcome To My Bathroom

Your Name Please

....

estimated weight of your  :

[..........] Grams   [.......] Pounds

Gender

☐   ☐   ☐ Rather Not Say

Date of Visit: ....

Time of Visit: ....

Length of Visit ....
(Mins):

Your Thoughts and your feelings

During Your Visit, Did You:

☐ Look At Your Poop

☐ Browsing Your Phone

☐ Miss It

☐ Put Down The Cover

☐ Used More Than Half Roll Of Paper

☐ Wash Your Hand

Welcome To My Bathroom

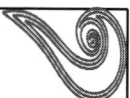

Your Name Please

....

Gender

☐ ☐ ☐ *Rather Not Say*

Date of Visit: ....

Time of Visit: ....

Length of Visit ....
(Mins):

During Your Visit, Did You:

☐ Look At Your **Poop**

☐ Browsing Your Phone

☐ *Miss It*

☐ Put Down The Cover

☐ Used More Than Half Roll Of Paper

☐ *Wash Your Hand*

estimated weight of your 💩 :

☐........ Grams   ☐....... Pounds

Your Thoughts and your feelings

....
....
....
....
....
....
....
....
....
....
....
....
....
....
....
....
....
....
....
....
....
....
....
....
....
....
....
....
....
....

Welcome To My Bathroom

Your Name Please

....

Gender

☐   ☐   ☐ Rather Not Say

Date of Visit: ·······························

Time of Visit: ·······························

Length of Visit ·······················
(Mins):

During Your Visit, Did You:

☐ Look At Your Poop

☐ Browsing Your Phone

☐ Miss It

☐ Put Down The Cover

☐ Used More Than Half Roll Of Paper

☐ Wash Your Hand

estimated weight of your 💩:

[.........] Grams   [.......] Pounds

Your Thoughts and your feelings

....
....
....
....
....
....
....
....
....
....
....
....
....
....
....
....
....
....
....
....
....
....
....
....
....
....
....
....
....

Welcome To My Bathroom

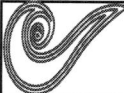
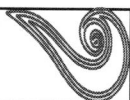

Your Name Please

....

Gender

☐ ☐ ☐ Rather Not Say

Date of Visit: ....

Time of Visit: ....

Length of Visit ....
(Mins):

During Your Visit, Did You:

☐ Look At Your *Poop*

☐ Browsing Your Phone

☐ *Miss It*

☐ Put Down The Cover

☐ Used More Than Half Roll Of Paper

☐ *Wash Your Hand*

estimated weight of your 💩 :

[.........] Grams   [.........] Pounds

Your Thoughts and your feelings

....
....
....
....
....
....
....
....
....
....
....
....
....
....
....
....
....
....
....
....
....
....
....
....
....
....
....
....
....
....
....
....
....

 # Welcome To My Bathroom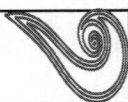

Your Name Please

....

Gender

☐ ☐ ☐ Rather Not Say

Date of Visit: ·······················

Time of Visit: ·······················

Length of Visit ·················
(Mins):

During Your Visit, Did You:

☐ Look At Your **Poop**

☐ Browsing Your Phone

☐ *Miss It*

☐ Put Down The Cover

☐ Used More Than Half Roll Of Paper

☐ Wash Your Hand

estimated weight of your 💩 :

☐......... Grams   ☐....... Pounds

Your Thoughts and your feelings

....
....
....
....
....
....
....
....
....
....
....
....
....
....
....
....
....
....
....
....
....
....
....
....
....
....
....
....
....
....
....
....
....

Welcome To My Bathroom

Your Name Please

....

Gender

☐ 👤 ☐ 👤 ☐ *Rather Not Say*

Date of Visit: ························

Time of Visit: ························

Length of Visit ····················
(Mins):

During Your Visit, Did You:

☐ Look At Your *Poop*

☐ *Browsing Your Phone*

☐ *Miss It*

☐ Put Down The Cover

☐ Used More Than Half Roll Of Paper

☐ *Wash Your Hand*

estimated weight of your 💩 :

☐········ Grams   ☐······· Pounds

Your Thoughts and your feelings

....
....
....
....
....
....
....
....
....
....
....
....
....
....
....
....
....
....
....
....
....
....
....
....
....
....
....
....

Welcome To My Bathroom

Your Name Please

....

Gender

☐   ☐   ☐ Rather Not Say

Date of Visit: ·····························

Time of Visit: ·····························

Length of Visit ·····················
(Mins):

During Your Visit, Did You:

☐ Look At Your **Poop**

☐ Browsing Your Phone

☐ *Miss It*

☐ Put Down The Cover

☐ Used More Than Half Roll Of Paper

☐ Wash Your Hand

estimated weight of your 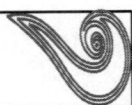 :

☐........ Grams   ☐....... Pounds

Your Thoughts and your feelings

....
....
....
....
....
....
....
....
....
....
....
....
....
....
....
....
....
....
....
....
....
....
....
....
....
....
....

Welcome To My Bathroom

Your Name Please
....

Gender

☐   ☐   ☐ Rather Not Say

Date of Visit: ································

Time of Visit: ································

Length of Visit ····················
(Mins):

During Your Visit, Did You:

☐ Look At Your **Poop**

☐ Browsing Your Phone

☐ *Miss It*

☐ Put Down The Cover

☐ Used More Than Half Roll Of Paper

☐ **Wash Your Hand**

estimated weight of your  :

┌·········┐ Grams   ┌·······┐ Pounds

Your Thoughts and your feelings
....
....
....
....
....
....
....
....
....
....
....
....
....
....
....
....
....
....
....
....
....
....
....
....
....
....
....
....

 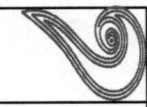

Welcome To My Bathroom

Your Name Please

....

Gender

☐ ☐ ☐ Rather Not Say

Date of Visit: ···

Time of Visit: ···

Length of Visit ···························
(Mins):

During Your Visit, Did You:

☐ Look At Your Poop

☐ Browsing Your Phone

☐ Miss It

☐ Put Down The Cover

☐ Used More Than Half Roll Of Paper

☐ Wash Your Hand

estimated weight of your 💩 :

☐ .... Grams   ☐ .... Pounds

Your Thoughts and your feelings

....
....
....
....
....
....
....
....
....
....
....
....
....
....
....
....
....
....
....
....
....
....
....
....
....
....
....
....

Welcome To My Bathroom

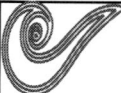 

Your Name Please

....

Gender

☐ ☐ ☐ Rather Not Say

Date of Visit: ································

Time of Visit: ································

Length of Visit ··················
(Mins):

During Your Visit, Did You:

☐ Look At Your *Poop*

☐ Browsing Your Phone

☐ *Miss It*

☐ Put Down The Cover

☐ Used More Than Half Roll Of Paper

☐ Wash Your Hand

estimated weight of your 💩:

[·········] Grams   [·······] Pounds

Your Thoughts and your feelings

....
....
....
....
....
....
....
....
....
....
....
....
....
....
....
....
....
....
....
....
....
....
....
....
....
....
....
....
....

Welcome To My Bathroom

Your Name Please

....

Gender

☐ ☐ ☐ Rather Not Say

Date of Visit: ·······························

Time of Visit: ·······························

Length of Visit ·······························
(Mins):

During Your Visit, Did You:

☐ Look At Your **Poop**

☐ Browsing Your Phone

☐ *Miss It*

☐ Put Down The Cover

☐ Used More Than Half Roll Of Paper

☐ **Wash Your Hand**

estimated weight of your 💩 :

[.........] Grams   [.......] Pounds

Your Thoughts and your feelings

....
....
....
....
....
....
....
....
....
....
....
....
....
....
....
....
....
....
....
....
....
....
....
....
....
....
....
....
....

Welcome To My Bathroom

 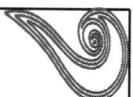

Your Name Please

....

estimated weight of your 💩:

[........] Grams   [........] Pounds

Gender

☐ 👩 ☐ 👨 ☐ Rather Not Say

Your Thoughts and your feelings

Date of Visit:·····························

Time of Visit:·····························

Length of Visit ·······················
(Mins):

During Your Visit, Did You:

☐ Look At Your *Poop*

☐ Browsing Your Phone

☐ *Miss It*

☐ Put Down The Cover

☐ Used More Than Half Roll Of Paper

☐ Wash Your Hand

Welcome To My Bathroom

Your Name Please

....

Gender

☐   ☐   ☐ Rather Not Say

Date of Visit: ·······················

Time of Visit: ·······················

Length of Visit ······················
(Mins):

During Your Visit, Did You:

☐ Look At Your *Poop*

☐ Browsing Your Phone

☐ *Miss It*

☐ Put Down The Cover

☐ Used More Than Half Roll Of Paper

☐ *Wash Your Hand*

estimated weight of your :

☐········ Grams   ☐······· Pounds

Your Thoughts and your feelings

....
....
....
....
....
....
....
....
....
....
....
....
....
....
....
....
....
....
....
....
....
....
....
....
....
....
....
....
....
....
....

Welcome To My Bathroom

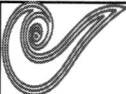
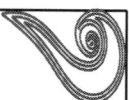

Your Name Please

....

Gender

☐   ☐   ☐ *Rather Not Say*

estimated weight of your 💩 :

☐....... *Grams*   ☐....... *Pounds*

Date of Visit:..........................

Time of Visit:..........................

Length of Visit ....
(Mins):

During Your Visit, Did You:

☐ Look At Your **Poop**

☐ Browsing Your Phone

☐ **Miss It**

☐ Put Down The Cover

☐ Used More Than Half Roll Of Paper

☐ **Wash Your Hand**

Your Thoughts and your feelings

....
....
....
....
....
....
....
....
....
....
....
....
....
....
....
....
....
....
....
....
....
....
....
....
....
....
....
....
....
....

Welcome To My Bathroom

Your Name Please

....

Gender

□   □   □ Rather Not Say

Date of Visit: ·······················

Time of Visit: ·······················

Length of Visit ·······················
(Mins):

During Your Visit, Did You:

□ Look At Your *Poop*

□ Browsing Your Phone

□ *Miss It*

□ Put Down The Cover

□ Used More Than Half Roll Of Paper

□ *Wash Your Hand*

estimated weight of your 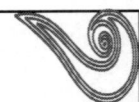 :

[........] Grams   [.......] Pounds

Your Thoughts and your feelings

....
....
....
....
....
....
....
....
....
....
....
....
....
....
....
....
....
....
....
....
....
....
....
....
....
....

Welcome To My Bathroom

 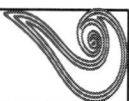

Your Name Please

....

Gender

☐   ☐   ☐ *Rather Not Say*

Date of Visit: ·································

Time of Visit: ·································

Length of Visit (Mins): ························

During Your Visit, Did You:

☐ Look At Your **Poop**

☐ Browsing Your Phone

☐ *Miss It*

☐ Put Down The Cover

☐ Used More Than Half Roll Of Paper

☐ Wash Your Hand

estimated weight of your 💩 :

☐········☐ Grams   ☐········☐ Pounds

Your Thoughts and your feelings

....
....
....
....
....
....
....
....
....
....
....
....
....
....
....
....
....
....
....
....
....
....
....
....
....
....
....
....
....

Welcome To My Bathroom

Your Name Please

....

Gender

☐   ☐   ☐ Rather Not Say

Date of Visit: ....

Time of Visit: ....

Length of Visit ....
(Mins):

During Your Visit, Did You:

☐ Look At Your **Poop**

☐ Browsing Your Phone

☐ *Miss It*

☐ Put Down The Cover

☐ Used More Than Half Roll Of Paper

☐ **Wash Your Hand**

estimated weight of your  :

☐........ Grams   ☐....... Pounds

Your Thoughts and your feelings

....
....
....
....
....
....
....
....
....
....
....
....
....
....
....
....
....
....
....
....
....
....
....
....
....
....
....
....

Welcome To My Bathroom

Your Name Please

....

Gender

☐ ☐ ☐ Rather Not Say

Date of Visit: ····························

Time of Visit: ····························

Length of Visit ····················
(Mins):

During Your Visit, Did You:

☐ Look At Your *Poop*

☐ Browsing Your Phone

☐ *Miss It*

☐ Put Down The Cover

☐ Used More Than Half Roll Of Paper

☐ Wash Your Hand

estimated weight of your 💩 :

[........] Grams   [.......] Pounds

Your Thoughts and your feelings

....
....
....
....
....
....
....
....
....
....
....
....
....
....
....
....
....
....
....
....
....
....
....
....
....
....
....

Welcome To My Bathroom

Your Name Please

....

Gender

☐   ☐   ☐ *Rather Not Say*

Date of Visit: ·····························

Time of Visit: ·····························

Length of Visit ·····························
(Mins):

During Your Visit, Did You:

☐ *Look At Your* **Poop**

☐ *Browsing Your Phone*

☐ *Miss It*

☐ *Put Down The Cover*

☐ *Used More Than Half Roll Of Paper*

☐ *Wash Your Hand*

estimated weight of your 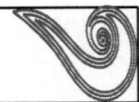 :

┌──────┐   Grams   ┌──────┐ Pounds
│........│   │.......│
└──────┘   └──────┘

Your Thoughts and your feelings

....
....
....
....
....
....
....
....
....
....
....
....
....
....
....
....
....
....
....
....
....
....
....
....
....
....
....
....

Welcome To My Bathroom

Your Name Please

....

Gender

☐ ☐ ☐ Rather Not Say

Date of Visit:·······················

Time of Visit:·····················

Length of Visit ····················
(Mins):

During Your Visit, Did You:

☐ Look At Your **Poop**

☐ Browsing Your Phone

☐ *Miss It*

☐ Put Down The Cover

☐ Used More Than Half Roll Of Paper

☐ **Wash Your Hand**

estimated weight of your 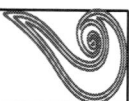 :

[········] Grams   [········] Pounds

Your Thoughts and your feelings

....
....
....
....
....
....
....
....
....
....
....
....
....
....
....
....
....
....
....
....
....
....
....
....
....
....
....
....
....

Welcome To My Bathroom

 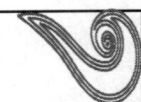

Your Name Please

....

Gender

□   □   □ *Rather Not Say*

Date of Visit: ··

Time of Visit: ··

Length of Visit ································
(Mins):

During Your Visit, Did You:

□ *Look At Your* **Poop**

□ *Browsing Your Phone*

□ *Miss It*

□ *Put Down The Cover*

□ *Used More Than Half Roll Of Paper*

□ *Wash Your Hand*

estimated weight of your 💩 :

[..........] *Grams*   [.......] *Pounds*

Your Thoughts and your feelings

....
....
....
....
....
....
....
....
....
....
....
....
....
....
....
....
....
....
....
....
....
....
....
....
....
....
....
....
....
....

Welcome To My Bathroom

Your Name Please

....

Gender

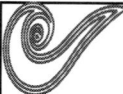

☐   ☐   ☐ Rather Not Say

Date of Visit: ·······················

Time of Visit: ·······················

Length of Visit ·····················
(Mins):

During Your Visit, Did You:

☐ Look At Your **Poop**

☐ Browsing Your Phone

☐ **Miss It**

☐ Put Down The Cover

☐ Used More Than Half Roll Of Paper

☐ **Wash Your Hand**

estimated weight of your 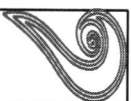 :

[········] Grams   [·······] Pounds

Your Thoughts and your feelings

....
....
....
....
....
....
....
....
....
....
....
....
....
....
....
....
....
....
....
....
....
....
....
....
....
....
....
....
....
....
....

Welcome To My Bathroom

Your Name Please

....

estimated weight of your 💩:

┌────────┐   ┌───────┐
│ ...... │ Grams   │ ..... │ Pounds
└────────┘   └───────┘

Gender

☐   ☐   ☐ Rather Not Say

Date of Visit: ··················

Time of Visit: ··················

Length of Visit ··················
(Mins):

Your Thoughts and your feelings

....
....
....
....
....
....
....
....
....
....
....
....
....
....
....
....
....
....
....
....
....
....
....
....
....
....
....
....
....
....
....
....
....

During Your Visit, Did You:

☐ Look At Your Poop

☐ Browsing Your Phone

☐ Miss It

☐ Put Down The Cover

☐ Used More Than Half Roll Of Paper

☐ Wash Your Hand

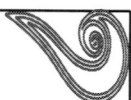

Welcome To My Bathroom

Your Name Please

....

Gender

☐   ☐   ☐ Rather Not Say

Date of Visit: ················

Time of Visit: ················

Length of Visit ·····················
(Mins):

During Your Visit, Did You:

☐ Look At Your **Poop**

☐ Browsing Your Phone

☐ **Miss It**

☐ Put Down The Cover

☐ Used More Than Half Roll Of Paper

☐ **Wash Your Hand**

estimated weight of your 💩 :

┌··········┐ Grams   ┌··········┐ Pounds
└··········┘   └··········┘

Your Thoughts and your feelings

....
....
....
....
....
....
....
....
....
....
....
....
....
....
....
....
....
....
....
....
....
....
....
....
....
....

Welcome To My Bathroom

 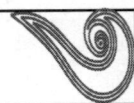

Your Name Please

....

estimated weight of your 💩 :

[.........] Grams   [.......] Pounds

Gender

☐ 👩‍💼   ☐ 👨‍💼   ☐ Rather Not Say

Date of Visit: ·················

Time of Visit: ·················

Length of Visit ·················
(Mins):

During Your Visit, Did You:

☐ Look At Your **Poop**

☐ Browsing Your Phone

☐ *Miss It*

☐ Put Down The Cover

☐ Used More Than Half Roll Of Paper

☐ *Wash Your Hand*

Your Thoughts and your feelings

....
....
....
....
....
....
....
....
....
....
....
....
....
....
....
....
....
....
....
....
....
....
....
....
....
....
....
....
....
....
....
....
....

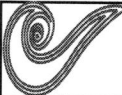 

Your Name Please

....

estimated weight of your 💩 :

[........] Grams   [.......] Pounds

Gender

☐   ☐   ☐ Rather Not Say

Your Thoughts and your feelings

Date of Visit: ·····························

Time of Visit: ·····························

Length of Visit ······················
(Mins):

During Your Visit, Did You:

☐ Look At Your **Poop**

☐ Browsing Your Phone

☐ *Miss It*

☐ Put Down The Cover

☐ Used More Than Half Roll Of Paper

☐ Wash Your Hand

Welcome To My Bathroom

Your Name Please

....

Gender

☐ ☐ ☐ Rather Not Say

Date of Visit: ....

Time of Visit: ....

Length of Visit ....
(Mins):

During Your Visit, Did You:

☐ Look At Your Poop

☐ Browsing Your Phone

☐ Miss It

☐ Put Down The Cover

☐ Used More Than Half Roll Of Paper

☐ Wash Your Hand

estimated weight of your 💩:

[.........] Grams   [.......] Pounds

Your Thoughts and your feelings

....
....
....
....
....
....
....
....
....
....
....
....
....
....
....
....
....
....
....
....
....
....
....
....
....
....
....
....

Welcome To My Bathroom

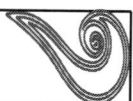

Your Name Please

....

Gender

☐ ☐ ☐ Rather Not Say

Date of Visit: ....

Time of Visit: ....

Length of Visit ....
(Mins):

During Your Visit, Did You:

☐ Look At Your **Poop**

☐ Browsing Your Phone

☐ *Miss It*

☐ Put Down The Cover

☐ Used More Than Half Roll Of Paper

☐ Wash Your Hand

estimated weight of your 💩 :

☐......... Grams   ☐....... Pounds

Your Thoughts and your feelings

....
....
....
....
....
....
....
....
....
....
....
....
....
....
....
....
....
....
....
....
....
....
....
....
....
....
....
....

Welcome To My Bathroom

Your Name Please

....

Gender

☐ ☐ ☐ Rather Not Say

Date of Visit: ....

Time of Visit: ....

Length of Visit ....
(Mins):

During Your Visit, Did You:

☐ Look At Your Poop

☐ Browsing Your Phone

☐ Miss It

☐ Put Down The Cover

☐ Used More Than Half Roll Of Paper

☐ Wash Your Hand

estimated weight of your 💩 :

[........] Grams   [........] Pounds

Your Thoughts and your feelings

....
....
....
....
....
....
....
....
....
....
....
....
....
....
....
....
....
....
....
....
....
....
....
....
....
....
....
....
....
....

Welcome To My Bathroom

Your Name Please

....

Gender

☐   ☐   ☐ *Rather Not Say*

estimated weight of your 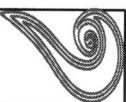 :

☐ .... *Grams*   ☐ .... *Pounds*

Date of Visit: ....

Time of Visit: ....

Length of Visit (Mins): ....

During Your Visit, Did You:

☐ *Look At Your Poop*

☐ *Browsing Your Phone*

☐ *Miss It*

☐ *Put Down The Cover*

☐ *Used More Than Half Roll Of Paper*

☐ *Wash Your Hand*

Your Thoughts and your feelings

....
....
....
....
....
....
....
....
....
....
....
....
....
....
....
....
....
....
....
....
....
....
....
....
....
....

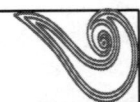

Your Name Please

....

Gender

☐ ☐ ☐ *Rather Not Say*

Date of Visit: ....

Time of Visit: ....

Length of Visit ....
(Mins):

During Your Visit, Did You:

☐ Look At Your **Poop**

☐ Browsing Your Phone

☐ *Miss It*

☐ Put Down The Cover

☐ Used More Than Half Roll Of Paper

☐ Wash Your Hand

estimated weight of your 💩 :

☐........ Grams   ☐....... Pounds

Your Thoughts and your feelings

....
....
....
....
....
....
....
....
....
....
....
....
....
....
....
....
....
....
....
....
....
....
....
....
....
....
....
....
....
....

Welcome To My Bathroom

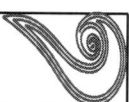

Your Name Please

....

Gender

☐   ☐   ☐ Rather Not Say

Date of Visit: ....

Time of Visit: ....

Length of Visit ....
(Mins):

During Your Visit, Did You:

☐ Look At Your **Poop**

☐ Browsing Your Phone

☐ *Miss It*

☐ Put Down The Cover

☐ Used More Than Half Roll Of Paper

☐ **Wash Your Hand**

estimated weight of your 💩 :

☐ .... Grams   ☐ .... Pounds

Your Thoughts and your feelings

....
....
....
....
....
....
....
....
....
....
....
....
....
....
....
....
....
....
....
....
....
....
....
....
....
....
....
....

Welcome To My Bathroom

Your Name Please

....

Gender

☐ ☐ ☐ Rather Not Say

Date of Visit: ···············

Time of Visit: ···············

Length of Visit (Mins): ···············

During Your Visit, Did You:

☐ Look At Your *Poop*

☐ Browsing Your Phone

☐ *Miss It*

☐ Put Down The Cover

☐ Used More Than Half Roll Of Paper

☐ *Wash Your Hand*

estimated weight of your  :

┌········┐ Grams ┌·······┐ Pounds

Your Thoughts and your feelings

....
....
....
....
....
....
....
....
....
....
....
....
....
....
....
....
....
....
....
....
....
....
....
....
....
....
....

Welcome To My Bathroom

Your Name Please

....

Gender

☐ 👩 ☐ 👨 ☐ Rather Not Say

Date of Visit: ···

Time of Visit: ···

Length of Visit ····························
(Mins):

During Your Visit, Did You:

☐ Look At Your **Poop**

☐ Browsing Your Phone

☐ *Miss It*

☐ Put Down The Cover

☐ Used More Than Half Roll Of Paper

☐ Wash Your Hand

estimated weight of your 💩 :

☐········· Grams   ☐······· Pounds

Your Thoughts and your feelings

....
....
....
....
....
....
....
....
....
....
....
....
....
....
....
....
....
....
....
....
....
....
....
....
....
....
....
....
....
....
....
....

Welcome To My Bathroom

 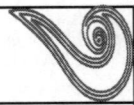

Your Name Please

....

Gender

☐ ☐ ☐ Rather Not Say

Date of Visit: ································

Time of Visit: ································

Length of Visit ·····················
(Mins):

During Your Visit, Did You:

☐ Look At Your **Poop**

☐ Browsing Your Phone

☐ *Miss It*

☐ Put Down The Cover

☐ Used More Than Half Roll Of Paper

☐ Wash Your Hand

estimated weight of your 💩 :

☐········ Grams   ☐······· Pounds

Your Thoughts and your feelings

....
....
....
....
....
....
....
....
....
....
....
....
....
....
....
....
....
....
....
....
....
....
....
....
....
....
....

Welcome To My Bathroom

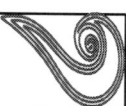

Your Name Please

....

Gender

☐ ☐ ☐ Rather Not Say

Date of Visit: ························

Time of Visit: ·························

Length of Visit ·····················
(Mins):

During Your Visit, Did You:

☐ Look At Your Poop

☐ Browsing Your Phone

☐ Miss It

☐ Put Down The Cover

☐ Used More Than Half Roll Of Paper

☐ Wash Your Hand

estimated weight of your 💩:

[.........] Grams   [.......] Pounds

Your Thoughts and your feelings

....
....
....
....
....
....
....
....
....
....
....
....
....
....
....
....
....
....
....
....
....
....
....
....
....
....

Welcome To My Bathroom

Your Name Please

....

Gender

☐ ☐ ☐ *Rather Not Say*

Date of Visit: ·······

Time of Visit: ·······

Length of Visit ··············
(Mins):

During Your Visit, Did You:

☐ *Look At Your* **Poop**

☐ *Browsing Your Phone*

☐ *Miss It*

☐ *Put Down The Cover*

☐ *Used More Than Half Roll Of Paper*

☐ **Wash Your Hand**

estimated weight of your 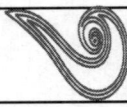 :

☐ .... *Grams*   ☐ .... *Pounds*

Your Thoughts and your feelings

....
....
....
....
....
....
....
....
....
....
....
....
....
....
....
....
....
....
....
....
....
....
....
....
....
....
....
....
....
....
....
....

Welcome To My Bathroom

Your Name Please

....

Gender

☐   ☐   ☐ Rather Not Say

Date of Visit: ································

Time of Visit: ································

Length of Visit ························
(Mins):

During Your Visit, Did You:

☐ Look At Your *Poop*

☐ Browsing Your Phone

☐ *Miss It*

☐ Put Down The Cover

☐ Used More Than Half Roll Of Paper

☐ *Wash Your Hand*

estimated weight of your  :

┌─────────┐   ┌─────────┐
│ .... │ Grams   │ .... │ Pounds
└─────────┘   └─────────┘

Your Thoughts and your feelings

....
....
....
....
....
....
....
....
....
....
....
....
....
....
....
....
....
....
....
....
....
....
....
....
....
....
....
....
....

Welcome To My Bathroom

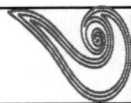

Your Name Please

....

Gender

☐ ☐ ☐ Rather Not Say

Date of Visit: ································

Time of Visit: ································

Length of Visit ························
(Mins):

During Your Visit, Did You:

☐ Look At Your **Poop**

☐ Browsing Your Phone

☐ *Miss It*

☐ Put Down The Cover

☐ Used More Than Half Roll Of Paper

☐ **Wash Your Hand**

estimated weight of your 💩 :

☐ ········ Grams   ☐ ······ Pounds

Your Thoughts and your feelings

....
....
....
....
....
....
....
....
....
....
....
....
....
....
....
....
....
....
....
....
....
....
....
....
....
....
....

Welcome To My Bathroom

 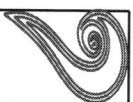

Your Name Please

....

Gender

☐ ☐ ☐ Rather Not Say

Date of Visit: ·····································

Time of Visit: ·····································

Length of Visit ·····························
(Mins):

During Your Visit, Did You:

☐ Look At Your **Poop**

☐ Browsing Your Phone

☐ *Miss It*

☐ Put Down The Cover

☐ Used More Than Half Roll Of Paper

☐ Wash Your Hand

estimated weight of your 💩 :

┌·········┐ Grams   ┌·······┐ Pounds
└─────────┘   └───────┘

Your Thoughts and your feelings

....
....
....
....
....
....
....
....
....
....
....
....
....
....
....
....
....
....
....
....
....
....
....
....
....
....
....
....
....

Welcome To My Bathroom

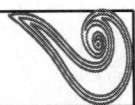

Your Name Please

....

Gender

☐ ☐ ☐ Rather Not Say

Date of Visit: ·······················

Time of Visit: ·······················

Length of Visit ·······················
(Mins):

During Your Visit, Did You:

☐ Look At Your *Poop*

☐ Browsing Your Phone

☐ *Miss It*

☐ Put Down The Cover

☐ Used More Than Half Roll Of Paper

☐ *Wash Your Hand*

---

estimated weight of your 💩 :

[.........] Grams   [.......] Pounds

Your Thoughts and your feelings

....
....
....
....
....
....
....
....
....
....
....
....
....
....
....
....
....
....
....
....
....
....
....
....
....
....
....

Welcome To My Bathroom

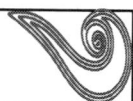

Your Name Please

....

Gender

☐   ☐   ☐ *Rather Not Say*

Date of Visit: ·····························

Time of Visit: ·····························

Length of Visit ·····················
(Mins):

During Your Visit, Did You:

☐ Look At Your **Poop**

☐ Browsing Your Phone

☐ *Miss It*

☐ Put Down The Cover

☐ Used More Than Half Roll Of Paper

☐ **Wash Your Hand**

estimated weight of your 💩 :

☐ ········· *Grams*   ☐ ······· *Pounds*

Your Thoughts and your feelings

....
....
....
....
....
....
....
....
....
....
....
....
....
....
....
....
....
....
....
....
....
....
....
....
....
....
....

Welcome To My Bathroom

Your Name Please

....

Gender

☐ ☐ ☐ Rather Not Say

Date of Visit: ....

Time of Visit: ....

Length of Visit ....
(Mins):

During Your Visit, Did You:

☐ Look At Your Poop

☐ Browsing Your Phone

☐ Miss It

☐ Put Down The Cover

☐ Used More Than Half Roll Of Paper

☐ Wash Your Hand

estimated weight of your  :

┌........┐ Grams   ┌........┐ Pounds

Your Thoughts and your feelings

....
....
....
....
....
....
....
....
....
....
....
....
....
....
....
....
....
....
....
....
....
....
....
....
....
....
....
....
....

Welcome To My Bathroom

Your Name Please

....

Gender

☐ ☐ ☐ Rather Not Say

Date of Visit: ....

Time of Visit: ....

Length of Visit ....
(Mins):

During Your Visit, Did You:

☐ Look At Your **Poop**

☐ Browsing Your Phone

☐ *Miss It*

☐ Put Down The Cover

☐ Used More Than Half Roll Of Paper

☐ Wash Your Hand

estimated weight of your  :

☐......... Grams   ☐........ Pounds

Your Thoughts and your feelings

....
....
....
....
....
....
....
....
....
....
....
....
....
....
....
....
....
....
....
....
....
....
....
....
....
....
....
....
....
....
....

Welcome To My Bathroom

Your Name Please

....

Gender

☐ ☐ ☐ Rather Not Say

estimated weight of your  **:**

| .... | Grams | | .... | Pounds |

Date of Visit: ....

Time of Visit: ....

Length of Visit ....
(Mins):

During Your Visit, Did You:

☐ Look At Your **Poop**

☐ Browsing Your Phone

☐ **Miss It**

☐ Put Down The Cover

☐ Used More Than Half Roll Of Paper

☐ **Wash Your Hand**

Your Thoughts and your feelings

....
....
....
....
....
....
....
....
....
....
....
....
....
....
....
....
....
....
....
....
....
....
....
....
....
....
....
....
....
....
....

Welcome To My Bathroom

Your Name Please

....

Gender

☐   ☐   ☐ Rather Not Say

Date of Visit: ....

Time of Visit: ....

Length of Visit ....
(Mins):

During Your Visit, Did You:

☐ Look At Your **Poop**

☐ Browsing Your Phone

☐ **Miss It**

☐ Put Down The Cover

☐ Used More Than Half Roll Of Paper

☐ **Wash Your Hand**

estimated weight of your 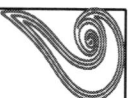 :

| .... Grams | .... Pounds |

Your Thoughts and your feelings

....
....
....
....
....
....
....
....
....
....
....
....
....
....
....
....
....
....
....
....
....
....
....
....
....
....
....
....
....
....
....
....

Welcome To My Bathroom

Your Name Please

....

estimated weight of your 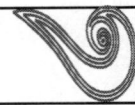 :

[........] Grams   [.......] Pounds

Gender

☐ ☐ ☐ Rather Not Say

Your Thoughts and your feelings

Date of Visit: ....

Time of Visit: ....

Length of Visit ....
(Mins):

During Your Visit, Did You:

☐ Look At Your **Poop**

☐ Browsing Your Phone

☐ *Miss It*

☐ Put Down The Cover

☐ Used More Than Half Roll Of Paper

☐ **Wash Your Hand**

Welcome To My Bathroom

Your Name Please

....

Gender

☐ ☐ ☐ Rather Not Say

Date of Visit: ·····················

Time of Visit: ·····················

Length of Visit ·····················
(Mins):

During Your Visit, Did You:

☐ Look At Your **Poop**

☐ Browsing Your Phone

☐ *Miss It*

☐ Put Down The Cover

☐ Used More Than Half Roll Of Paper

☐ Wash Your Hand

estimated weight of your  :

| .... | Grams | .... | Pounds |

Your Thoughts and your feelings

....
....
....
....
....
....
....
....
....
....
....
....
....
....
....
....
....
....
....
....
....
....
....
....
....
....

Welcome To My Bathroom

Your Name Please

....

Gender

☐ ☐ ☐ Rather Not Say

Date of Visit: ·············

Time of Visit: ·············

Length of Visit ·············
(Mins):

During Your Visit, Did You:

☐ Look At Your **Poop**

☐ Browsing Your Phone

☐ *Miss It*

☐ Put Down The Cover

☐ Used More Than Half Roll Of Paper

☐ **Wash Your Hand**

estimated weight of your 💩 :

[........] Grams   [.......] Pounds

Your Thoughts and your feelings

....
....
....
....
....
....
....
....
....
....
....
....
....
....
....
....
....
....
....
....
....
....
....
....
....
....
....
....
....
....
....

Welcome To My Bathroom

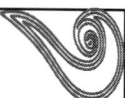

Your Name Please

....

Gender

☐ ☐ ☐ Rather Not Say

Date of Visit: ································

Time of Visit: ·····························

Length of Visit ·······················
(Mins):

During Your Visit, Did You:

☐ Look At Your **Poop**

☐ Browsing Your Phone

☐ *Miss It*

☐ Put Down The Cover

☐ Used More Than Half Roll Of Paper

☐ **Wash Your Hand**

estimated weight of your 💩 :

☐............☐ Grams   ☐.........☐ Pounds

Your Thoughts and your feelings

....
....
....
....
....
....
....
....
....
....
....
....
....
....
....
....
....
....
....
....
....
....
....
....
....
....
....
....

 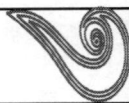

Your Name Please

....

Gender

☐   ☐   ☐ Rather Not Say

Date of Visit: ....

Time of Visit: ....

Length of Visit ....
(Mins):

During Your Visit, Did You:

☐ Look At Your **Poop**

☐ Browsing Your Phone

☐ *Miss It*

☐ Put Down The Cover

☐ Used More Than Half Roll Of Paper

☐ Wash Your Hand

estimated weight of your 💩 :

☐............ Grams   ☐......... Pounds

Your Thoughts and your feelings

....
....
....
....
....
....
....
....
....
....
....
....
....
....
....
....
....
....
....
....
....
....
....
....
....
....
....
....
....

Welcome To My Bathroom

Your Name Please

....

Gender

☐ ☐ ☐ Rather Not Say

Date of Visit: ·······················

Time of Visit: ·······················

Length of Visit ····················
(Mins):

During Your Visit, Did You:

☐ Look At Your **Poop**

☐ Browsing Your Phone

☐ **Miss It**

☐ Put Down The Cover

☐ Used More Than Half Roll Of Paper

☐ **Wash Your Hand**

estimated weight of your 💩 :

[........] Grams   [......] Pounds

Your Thoughts and your feelings

....
....
....
....
....
....
....
....
....
....
....
....
....
....
....
....
....
....
....
....
....
....
....
....
....
....
....
....
....
....

Welcome To My Bathroom

Your Name Please

....

Gender

☐   ☐   ☐ Rather Not Say

Date of Visit: ·································

Time of Visit: ·································

Length of Visit ·······················
(Mins):

During Your Visit, Did You:

☐ Look At Your **Poop**

☐ Browsing Your Phone

☐ *Miss It*

☐ Put Down The Cover

☐ Used More Than Half Roll Of Paper

☐ *Wash Your Hand*

estimated weight of your  :

☐ .... Grams   ☐ .... Pounds

Your Thoughts and your feelings

....
....
....
....
....
....
....
....
....
....
....
....
....
....
....
....
....
....
....
....
....
....
....
....
....
....
....
....
....
....

Welcome To My Bathroom

Your Name Please

....

Gender

☐   ☐   ☐ Rather Not Say

Date of Visit: ....

Time of Visit: ....

Length of Visit (Mins): ....

During Your Visit, Did You:

☐ Look At Your **Poop**

☐ Browsing Your Phone

☐ *Miss It*

☐ Put Down The Cover

☐ Used More Than Half Roll Of Paper

☐ **Wash Your Hand**

estimated weight of your  :

☐ .... Grams   ☐ .... Pounds

Your Thoughts and your feelings

....
....
....
....
....
....
....
....
....
....
....
....
....
....
....
....
....
....
....
....
....
....
....
....
....
....
....
....

Welcome To My Bathroom

Your Name Please

....

Gender

☐ ☐ ☐ Rather Not Say

Date of Visit: ························

Time of Visit: ························

Length of Visit ························
(Mins):

During Your Visit, Did You:

☐ Look At Your **Poop**

☐ Browsing Your Phone

☐ *Miss It*

☐ Put Down The Cover

☐ Used More Than Half Roll Of Paper

☐ Wash Your Hand

estimated weight of your :

┌········┐ Grams   ┌······┐ Pounds

Your Thoughts and your feelings

....
....
....
....
....
....
....
....
....
....
....
....
....
....
....
....
....
....
....
....
....
....
....
....
....
....
....
....
....
....

Welcome To My Bathroom

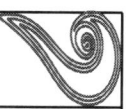

Your Name Please

....

Gender

☐   ☐   ☐ Rather Not Say

Date of Visit: ······················

Time of Visit: ······················

Length of Visit ·····················
(Mins):

During Your Visit, Did You:

☐ Look At Your *Poop*

☐ Browsing Your Phone

☐ *Miss It*

☐ Put Down The Cover

☐ Used More Than Half Roll Of Paper

☐ Wash Your Hand

estimated weight of your 💩 :

☐········ Grams   ☐······ Pounds

Your Thoughts and your feelings

....
....
....
....
....
....
....
....
....
....
....
....
....
....
....
....
....
....
....
....
....
....
....
....
....
....
....
....

Welcome To My Bathroom

Your Name Please

....

Gender

☐   ☐   ☐ Rather Not Say

Date of Visit:·············

Time of Visit:·············

Length of Visit ··················
(Mins):

During Your Visit, Did You:

☐ Look At Your *Poop*

☐ Browsing Your Phone

☐ *Miss It*

☐ Put Down The Cover

☐ Used More Than Half Roll Of Paper

☐ *Wash Your Hand*

estimated weight of your 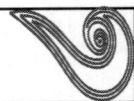 :

[········] Grams   [·······] Pounds

Your Thoughts and your feelings

....
....
....
....
....
....
....
....
....
....
....
....
....
....
....
....
....
....
....
....
....
....
....
....
....
....
....
....
....
....

Welcome To My Bathroom

Your Name Please

....

Gender

 ☐   ☐ 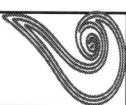   ☐ Rather Not Say

Date of Visit: ....

Time of Visit: ....

Length of Visit ....
(Mins):

During Your Visit, Did You:

☐ Look At Your **Poop**

☐ Browsing Your Phone

☐ *Miss It*

☐ Put Down The Cover

☐ Used More Than Half Roll Of Paper

☐ Wash Your Hand

estimated weight of your 💩:

┌──────┐ Grams   ┌──────┐ Pounds
└──────┘   └──────┘

Your Thoughts and your feelings

....
....
....
....
....
....
....
....
....
....
....
....
....
....
....
....
....
....
....
....
....
....
....
....
....
....
....
....
....

Welcome To My Bathroom

Your Name Please

....

Gender

☐   ☐   ☐ Rather Not Say

Date of Visit: ·············

Time of Visit: ·············

Length of Visit ·············
(Mins):

During Your Visit, Did You:

☐ Look At Your **Poop**

☐ Browsing Your Phone

☐ *Miss It*

☐ Put Down The Cover

☐ Used More Than Half Roll Of Paper

☐ **Wash Your Hand**

estimated weight of your  :

[........] Grams   [.......] Pounds

Your Thoughts and your feelings

....
....
....
....
....
....
....
....
....
....
....
....
....
....
....
....
....
....
....
....
....
....
....
....
....
....
....
....
....
....

Welcome To My Bathroom

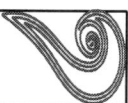

Your Name Please

....

Gender

☐ ☐ ☐ Rather Not Say

Date of Visit:····················

Time of Visit:····················

Length of Visit ·····················
(Mins):

During Your Visit, Did You:

☐ Look At Your **Poop**

☐ Browsing Your Phone

☐ *Miss It*

☐ Put Down The Cover

☐ Used More Than Half Roll Of Paper

☐ **Wash Your Hand**

estimated weight of your 💩 :

[·········] Grams   [·······] Pounds

Your Thoughts and your feelings

....
....
....
....
....
....
....
....
....
....
....
....
....
....
....
....
....
....
....
....
....
....
....
....
....

Welcome To My Bathroom

Your Name Please

....

Gender

☐   ☐   ☐ Rather Not Say

Date of Visit: ·····································

Time of Visit: ·····································

Length of Visit ·····························
(Mins):

During Your Visit, Did You:

☐ Look At Your **Poop**

☐ Browsing Your Phone

☐ *Miss It*

☐ Put Down The Cover

☐ Used More Than Half Roll Of Paper

☐ *Wash Your Hand*

estimated weight of your  :

☐........ Grams   ☐....... Pounds

Your Thoughts and your feelings

....
....
....
....
....
....
....
....
....
....
....
....
....
....
....
....
....
....
....
....
....
....
....
....
....
....
....
....
....
....
....

Welcome To My Bathroom

Your Name Please

....

Gender

 ☐ ☐ 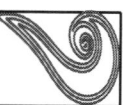 ☐ *Rather Not Say*

Date of Visit: ·····························

Time of Visit: ·····························

Length of Visit ····························
(Mins):

During Your Visit, Did You:

☐ Look At Your **Poop**

☐ Browsing Your Phone

☐ *Miss It*

☐ Put Down The Cover

☐ Used More Than Half Roll Of Paper

☐ Wash Your Hand

estimated weight of your 💩 :

☐········ Grams   ☐······· Pounds

Your Thoughts and your feelings

....
....
....
....
....
....
....
....
....
....
....
....
....
....
....
....
....
....
....
....
....
....
....
....
....
....
....
....
....

Welcome To My Bathroom

Your Name Please

....

Gender

☐   ☐   ☐ Rather Not Say

Date of Visit:.........................

Time of Visit:.........................

Length of Visit ....
(Mins):

During Your Visit, Did You:

☐ Look At Your **Poop**

☐ Browsing Your Phone

☐ *Miss It*

☐ Put Down The Cover

☐ Used More Than Half Roll Of Paper

☐ Wash Your Hand

estimated weight of your 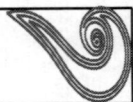 :

| .... | Grams | .... | Pounds |

Your Thoughts and your feelings

....
....
....
....
....
....
....
....
....
....
....
....
....
....
....
....
....
....
....
....
....
....
....
....
....
....
....
....
....
....

Welcome To My Bathroom

Your Name Please

....

Gender

☐ ☐ ☐ Rather Not Say

Date of Visit: ·······························

Time of Visit: ·······························

Length of Visit ························
(Mins):

During Your Visit, Did You:

☐ Look At Your *Poop*

☐ Browsing Your Phone

☐ *Miss It*

☐ Put Down The Cover

☐ Used More Than Half Roll Of Paper

☐ *Wash Your Hand*

estimated weight of your  :

☐......... Grams ☐....... Pounds

Your Thoughts and your feelings

....
....
....
....
....
....
....
....
....
....
....
....
....
....
....
....
....
....
....
....
....
....
....
....
....
....
....
....
....

Welcome To My Bathroom

Your Name Please

....

Gender

☐ ☐ ☐ Rather Not Say

Date of Visit: ....

Time of Visit: ....

Length of Visit ....
(Mins):

During Your Visit, Did You:

☐ Look At Your **Poop**

☐ Browsing Your Phone

☐ *Miss It*

☐ Put Down The Cover

☐ Used More Than Half Roll Of Paper

☐ Wash Your Hand

estimated weight of your 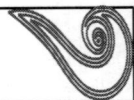 :

☐ .... Grams   ☐ .... Pounds

Your Thoughts and your feelings

....
....
....
....
....
....
....
....
....
....
....
....
....
....
....
....
....
....
....
....
....
....
....
....
....
....
....
....
....

Welcome To My Bathroom

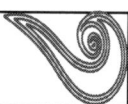

Your Name Please

....

Gender

☐ 👩 ☐ 👨 ☐ Rather Not Say

Date of Visit: ·············

Time of Visit: ·············

Length of Visit ··············
(Mins):

During Your Visit, Did You:

☐ Look At Your *Poop*

☐ Browsing Your Phone

☐ *Miss It*

☐ Put Down The Cover

☐ Used More Than Half Roll Of Paper

☐ Wash Your Hand

estimated weight of your 💩 :

[..........] Grams   [.......] Pounds

Your Thoughts and your feelings

....
....
....
....
....
....
....
....
....
....
....
....
....
....
....
....
....
....
....
....
....
....
....
....
....
....
....
....
....
....
....

Welcome To My Bathroom

Your Name Please

....

Gender

☐ ☐ ☐ Rather Not Say

Date of Visit: ·······················

Time of Visit: ·······················

Length of Visit ·······················
(Mins):

During Your Visit, Did You:

☐ Look At Your **Poop**

☐ Browsing Your Phone

☐ **Miss It**

☐ Put Down The Cover

☐ Used More Than Half Roll Of Paper

☐ **Wash Your Hand**

estimated weight of your  :

☐......... Grams   ☐....... Pounds

Your Thoughts and your feelings

....
....
....
....
....
....
....
....
....
....
....
....
....
....
....
....
....
....
....
....
....
....
....
....
....
....
....
....
....
....
....

Welcome To My Bathroom

 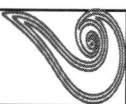

Your Name Please

....

Gender

☐ ☐ ☐ Rather Not Say

Date of Visit: ·····························

Time of Visit: ·····························

Length of Visit ·····················
(Mins):

During Your Visit, Did You:

☐ Look At Your **Poop**

☐ Browsing Your Phone

☐ *Miss It*

☐ Put Down The Cover

☐ Used More Than Half Roll Of Paper

☐ Wash Your Hand

estimated weight of your 💩:

[........] Grams   [......] Pounds

Your Thoughts and your feelings

....
....
....
....
....
....
....
....
....
....
....
....
....
....
....
....
....
....
....
....
....
....
....
....
....
....

Welcome To My Bathroom

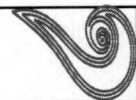

Your Name Please

....

Gender

☐ ☐ ☐ Rather Not Say

Date of Visit: ··································

Time of Visit: ·································

Length of Visit ····························
(Mins):

During Your Visit, Did You:

☐ Look At Your **Poop**

☐ Browsing Your Phone

☐ *Miss It*

☐ Put Down The Cover

☐ Used More Than Half Roll Of Paper

☐ **Wash Your Hand**

estimated weight of your 💩 :

[........] Grams   [.......] Pounds

Your Thoughts and your feelings

....
....
....
....
....
....
....
....
....
....
....
....
....
....
....
....
....
....
....
....
....
....
....
....
....
....
....
....
....

Welcome To My Bathroom

Your Name Please

....

Gender

☐   ☐   ☐ Rather Not Say

Date of Visit:..

Time of Visit:..

Length of Visit (Mins): ....

During Your Visit, Did You:

☐ Look At Your **Poop**

☐ Browsing Your Phone

☐ *Miss It*

☐ Put Down The Cover

☐ Used More Than Half Roll Of Paper

☐ **Wash Your Hand**

estimated weight of your 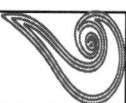 :

[..........] Grams   [.......] Pounds

Your Thoughts and your feelings

....
....
....
....
....
....
....
....
....
....
....
....
....
....
....
....
....
....
....
....
....
....
....
....
....
....

Welcome To My Bathroom

Your Name Please

....

Gender

☐ 👤 ☐ 👤 ☐ Rather Not Say

Date of Visit: ....

Time of Visit: ....

Length of Visit ....
(Mins):

During Your Visit, Did You:

☐ Look At Your *Poop*

☐ Browsing Your Phone

☐ *Miss It*

☐ Put Down The Cover

☐ Used More Than Half Roll Of Paper

☐ Wash Your Hand

estimated weight of your 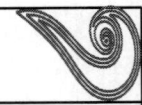 :

[........] Grams   [.......] Pounds

Your Thoughts and your feelings

....
....
....
....
....
....
....
....
....
....
....
....
....
....
....
....
....
....
....
....
....
....
....
....
....
....
....
....
....
....
....
....
....
....

Welcome To My Bathroom

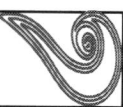

Your Name Please

....

Gender

☐   ☐   ☐ *Rather Not Say*

Date of Visit: ·······························

Time of Visit: ·····························

Length of Visit ·······················
(Mins):

During Your Visit, Did You:

☐ *Look At Your* **Poop**

☐ *Browsing Your Phone*

☐ *Miss It*

☐ *Put Down The Cover*

☐ *Used More Than Half Roll Of Paper*

☐ *Wash Your Hand*

estimated weight of your 💩 :

☐·········· *Grams*   ☐········· *Pounds*

Your Thoughts and your feelings

....
....
....
....
....
....
....
....
....
....
....
....
....
....
....
....
....
....
....
....
....
....
....
....
....
....
....
....
....

Welcome To My Bathroom

Your Name Please

....

Gender

☐ ☐ ☐Rather Not Say

Date of Visit: ·············

Time of Visit: ·············

Length of Visit ·············
(Mins):

During Your Visit, Did You:

☐ Look At Your *Poop*

☐ Browsing Your Phone

☐ *Miss It*

☐ Put Down The Cover

☐ Used More Than Half Roll Of Paper

☐ *Wash Your Hand*

estimated weight of your 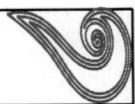 :

☐········ Grams   ☐······· Pounds

Your Thoughts and your feelings

....
....
....
....
....
....
....
....
....
....
....
....
....
....
....
....
....
....
....
....
....
....
....
....
....
....
....
....
....

Welcome To My Bathroom

Your Name Please

....

Gender

☐   ☐   ☐ Rather Not Say

Date of Visit: ························

Time of Visit: ························

Length of Visit ························
(Mins):

During Your Visit, Did You:

☐ Look At Your **Poop**

☐ Browsing Your Phone

☐ *Miss It*

☐ Put Down The Cover

☐ Used More Than Half Roll Of Paper

☐ Wash Your Hand

---

estimated weight of your 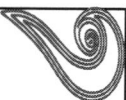 :

☐ .... Grams   ☐ .... Pounds

Your Thoughts and your feelings

....
....
....
....
....
....
....
....
....
....
....
....
....
....
....
....
....
....
....
....
....
....
....
....
....
....

Welcome To My Bathroom

Your Name Please

....

Gender

☐　　☐　　☐ Rather Not Say

Date of Visit: ··

Time of Visit: ··

Length of Visit ··································
(Mins):

During Your Visit, Did You:

☐ Look At Your *Poop*

☐ Browsing Your Phone

☐ *Miss It*

☐ Put Down The Cover

☐ Used More Than Half Roll Of Paper

☐ Wash Your Hand

estimated weight of your 💩 :

☐········ Grams ☐······· Pounds

Your Thoughts and your feelings

....
....
....
....
....
....
....
....
....
....
....
....
....
....
....
....
....
....
....
....
....
....
....
....
....
....
....
....
....
....

Welcome To My Bathroom

Your Name Please
....

Gender

☐ ☐ ☐ Rather Not Say

Date of Visit: ·······························

Time of Visit: ·······························

Length of Visit ·························
(Mins):

During Your Visit, Did You:

☐ Look At Your **Poop**

☐ Browsing Your Phone

☐ *Miss It*

☐ Put Down The Cover

☐ Used More Than Half Roll Of Paper

☐ Wash Your Hand

estimated weight of your  :

| .... | Grams | .... | Pounds |

Your Thoughts and your feelings
....
....
....
....
....
....
....
....
....
....
....
....
....
....
....
....
....
....
....
....
....
....
....
....
....

Welcome To My Bathroom

Your Name Please

....

Gender

☐ ☐ ☐Rather Not Say

Date of Visit: ⋯⋯⋯⋯⋯⋯⋯⋯⋯

Time of Visit: ⋯⋯⋯⋯⋯⋯⋯

Length of Visit ⋯⋯⋯⋯⋯⋯
(Mins):

During Your Visit, Did You:

☐ Look At Your **Poop**

☐ Browsing Your Phone

☐ *Miss It*

☐ Put Down The Cover

☐ Used More Than Half Roll Of Paper

☐ *Wash Your Hand*

estimated weight of your 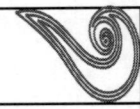 :

┌─────────┐   ┌─────────┐
│ .... │ Grams   │ .... │ Pounds
└─────────┘   └─────────┘

Your Thoughts and your feelings

....
....
....
....
....
....
....
....
....
....
....
....
....
....
....
....
....
....
....
....
....
....
....
....
....
....
....
....
....
....

Welcome To My Bathroom

 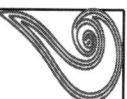

Your Name Please

....

estimated weight of your 💩 :

[..........] Grams   [.......] Pounds

Gender

☐   ☐   ☐ Rather Not Say

Your Thoughts and your feelings

....
....
....
....
....

Date of Visit: ....

....
....

Time of Visit: ....

....
....

Length of Visit ....
(Mins):

....
....
....

During Your Visit, Did You:

....
....
....
....

☐ Look At Your **Poop**

....

☐ Browsing Your Phone

....

☐ *Miss It*

....

☐ Put Down The Cover

....

☐ Used More Than Half Roll Of Paper

....

☐ Wash Your Hand

....
....
....
....

Welcome To My Bathroom

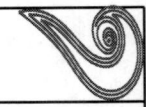

Your Name Please

....

Gender

☐ ☐ ☐Rather Not Say

Date of Visit:··

Time of Visit:···

Length of Visit ·······························
(Mins):

During Your Visit, Did You:

☐ Look At Your **Poop**

☐ Browsing Your Phone

☐ **Miss It**

☐ Put Down The Cover

☐ Used More Than Half Roll Of Paper

☐ **Wash Your Hand**

---

estimated weight of your 💩:

☐......... Grams   ☐....... Pounds

Your Thoughts and your feelings

....
....
....
....
....
....
....
....
....
....
....
....
....
....
....
....
....
....
....
....
....
....
....
....
....
....
....

Welcome To My Bathroom

Your Name Please

....

Gender

☐   ☐   ☐ *Rather Not Say*

Date of Visit: ·······························

Time of Visit: ·······························

Length of Visit ··················
(Mins):

During Your Visit, Did You:

☐ *Look At Your* **Poop**

☐ *Browsing Your Phone*

☐ *Miss It*

☐ *Put Down The Cover*

☐ *Used More Than Half Roll Of Paper*

☐ *Wash Your Hand*

estimated weight of your  :

| .... | Grams | .... | Pounds |

Your Thoughts and your feelings

....
....
....
....
....
....
....
....
....
....
....
....
....
....
....
....
....
....
....
....
....
....
....
....
....
....

Welcome To My Bathroom

Your Name Please

....

Gender

☐ ☐ ☐ Rather Not Say

Date of Visit: ·······························

Time of Visit: ·······························

Length of Visit ························
(Mins):

During Your Visit, Did You:

☐ Look At Your **Poop**

☐ Browsing Your Phone

☐ *Miss It*

☐ Put Down The Cover

☐ Used More Than Half Roll Of Paper

☐ Wash Your Hand

estimated weight of your 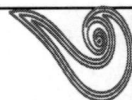 :

[..........] Grams   [.......] Pounds

Your Thoughts and your feelings

....
....
....
....
....
....
....
....
....
....
....
....
....
....
....
....
....
....
....
....
....
....
....
....
....
....
....
....
....
....

Welcome To My Bathroom

Your Name Please

....

Gender

☐ ☐ ☐ Rather Not Say

Date of Visit: ···························

Time of Visit: ···························

Length of Visit ·····················
(Mins):

During Your Visit, Did You:

☐ Look At Your **Poop**

☐ Browsing Your Phone

☐ *Miss It*

☐ Put Down The Cover

☐ Used More Than Half Roll Of Paper

☐ Wash Your Hand

estimated weight of your 💩 :

☐ ········· Grams   ☐ ······· Pounds

Your Thoughts and your feelings

....
....
....
....
....
....
....
....
....
....
....
....
....
....
....
....
....
....
....
....
....
....
....
....
....
....
....
....
....
....

Welcome To My Bathroom

Your Name Please

....

Gender

☐ ☐ ☐ Rather Not Say

Date of Visit: ·················

Time of Visit: ·················

Length of Visit (Mins): ·················

During Your Visit, Did You:

☐ Look At Your *Poop*

☐ Browsing Your Phone

☐ *Miss It*

☐ Put Down The Cover

☐ Used More Than Half Roll Of Paper

☐ *Wash Your Hand*

estimated weight of your 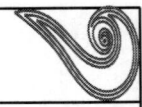 :

| .... | Grams | .... | Pounds |

Your Thoughts and your feelings

....
....
....
....
....
....
....
....
....
....
....
....
....
....
....
....
....
....
....
....
....
....
....
....
....
....
....
....
....
....
....

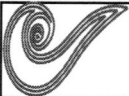

Welcome To My Bathroom

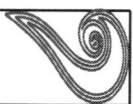

Your Name Please

....

Gender

☐   ☐   ☐ Rather Not Say

Date of Visit: ·····························

Time of Visit: ·····························

Length of Visit ·····················
(Mins):

During Your Visit, Did You:

☐ Look At Your *Poop*

☐ Browsing Your Phone

☐ *Miss It*

☐ Put Down The Cover

☐ Used More Than Half Roll Of Paper

☐ *Wash Your Hand*

estimated weight of your 💩 :

☐ ········ Grams   ☐ ······· Pounds

Your Thoughts and your feelings

....
....
....
....
....
....
....
....
....
....
....
....
....
....
....
....
....
....
....
....
....
....
....
....
....
....
....
....
....
....
....
....
....

Welcome To My Bathroom

Your Name Please

....

Gender

☐   ☐   ☐ Rather Not Say

Date of Visit: ·······················

Time of Visit: ·······················

Length of Visit (Mins): ·······················

During Your Visit, Did You:

☐ Look At Your *Poop*

☐ Browsing Your Phone

☐ *Miss It*

☐ Put Down The Cover

☐ Used More Than Half Roll Of Paper

☐ *Wash Your Hand*

---

estimated weight of your 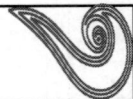 :

☐········· Grams   ☐······· Pounds

Your Thoughts and your feelings

....
....
....
....
....
....
....
....
....
....
....
....
....
....
....
....
....
....
....
....
....
....
....
....

Welcome To My Bathroom

 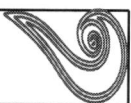

Your Name Please

....

Gender

☐ ☐ ☐ Rather Not Say

Date of Visit: ·······························

Time of Visit: ·······························

Length of Visit ·······························
(Mins):

During Your Visit, Did You:

☐ Look At Your **Poop**

☐ Browsing Your Phone

☐ *Miss It*

☐ Put Down The Cover

☐ Used More Than Half Roll Of Paper

☐ Wash Your Hand

estimated weight of your 💩 :

☐········· Grams   ☐······· Pounds

Your Thoughts and your feelings

....
....
....
....
....
....
....
....
....
....
....
....
....
....
....
....
....
....
....
....
....
....
....
....
....
....
....
....

Welcome To My Bathroom

Your Name Please

....

Gender

☐   ☐   ☐ Rather Not Say

Date of Visit: ·················

Time of Visit: ·················

Length of Visit (Mins): ·················

During Your Visit, Did You:

☐ Look At Your **Poop**

☐ Browsing Your Phone

☐ *Miss It*

☐ Put Down The Cover

☐ Used More Than Half Roll Of Paper

☐ *Wash Your Hand*

estimated weight of your  :

☐......... Grams   ☐....... Pounds

Your Thoughts and your feelings

....
....
....
....
....
....
....
....
....
....
....
....
....
....
....
....
....
....
....
....
....
....
....
....
....
....
....

Welcome To My Bathroom

Your Name Please

....

Gender

□ ☐ □ ☐ ☐ Rather Not Say

Date of Visit: ....

Time of Visit: ....

Length of Visit ....
(Mins):

During Your Visit, Did You:

☐ Look At Your **Poop**

☐ Browsing Your Phone

☐ *Miss It*

☐ Put Down The Cover

☐ Used More Than Half Roll Of Paper

☐ Wash Your Hand

estimated weight of your 💩 :

[..........] Grams   [.......] Pounds

Your Thoughts and your feelings

....
....
....
....
....
....
....
....
....
....
....
....
....
....
....
....
....
....
....
....
....
....
....
....
....
....
....
....

Welcome To My Bathroom

Your Name Please

....

Gender

☐   ☐   ☐ Rather Not Say

Date of Visit: ································

Time of Visit: ································

Length of Visit ·······························
(Mins):

During Your Visit, Did You:

☐ Look At Your *Poop*

☐ Browsing Your Phone

☐ *Miss It*

☐ Put Down The Cover

☐ Used More Than Half Roll Of Paper

☐ *Wash Your Hand*

estimated weight of your 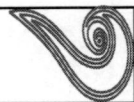 :

[.........] Grams   [.......] Pounds

Your Thoughts and your feelings

....
....
....
....
....
....
....
....
....
....
....
....
....
....
....
....
....
....
....
....
....
....
....
....
....
....
....
....
....

Welcome To My Bathroom

Your Name Please

....

Gender

☐ ☐ ☐ Rather Not Say

Date of Visit: ···································

Time of Visit: ···································

Length of Visit ···························
(Mins):

During Your Visit, Did You:

☐ Look At Your **Poop**

☐ Browsing Your Phone

☐ *Miss It*

☐ Put Down The Cover

☐ Used More Than Half Roll Of Paper

☐ Wash Your Hand

---

estimated weight of your 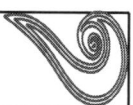 :

☐........ Grams   ☐....... Pounds

Your Thoughts and your feelings

....
....
....
....
....
....
....
....
....
....
....
....
....
....
....
....
....
....
....
....
....
....
....
....
....
....
....
....

Welcome To My Bathroom

Your Name Please
....

Gender

☐ ☐ ☐ Rather Not Say

Date of Visit: ··································

Time of Visit: ··································

Length of Visit ··························
(Mins):

During Your Visit, Did You:

☐ Look At Your **Poop**

☐ Browsing Your Phone

☐ *Miss It*

☐ Put Down The Cover

☐ Used More Than Half Roll Of Paper

☐ Wash Your Hand

estimated weight of your  :

[..........] Grams   [........] Pounds

Your Thoughts and your feelings

....
....
....
....
....
....
....
....
....
....
....
....
....
....
....
....
....
....
....
....
....
....
....
....
....
....
....
....

Welcome To My Bathroom

Your Name Please

....

Gender

☐ 　☐ 　☐ Rather Not Say

Date of Visit: ······························

Time of Visit: ······························

Length of Visit ························
(Mins):

During Your Visit, Did You:

☐ Look At Your **Poop**

☐ Browsing Your Phone

☐ *Miss It*

☐ Put Down The Cover

☐ Used More Than Half Roll Of Paper

☐ *Wash Your Hand*

---

estimated weight of your 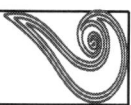 :

☐ .... Grams 　　☐ .... Pounds

Your Thoughts and your feelings

....
....
....
....
....
....
....
....
....
....
....
....
....
....
....
....
....
....
....
....
....
....
....
....
....
....
....

Welcome To My Bathroom

Your Name Please

....

estimated weight of your 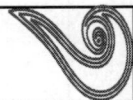 :

[........] Grams   [.......] Pounds

Gender

☐   ☐   ☐ Rather Not Say

Your Thoughts and your feelings

Date of Visit: ....

Time of Visit: ....

Length of Visit ....
(Mins):

During Your Visit, Did You:

☐ Look At Your **Poop**

☐ Browsing Your Phone

☐ *Miss It*

☐ Put Down The Cover

☐ Used More Than Half Roll Of Paper

☐ Wash Your Hand

Welcome To My Bathroom

 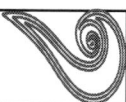

Your Name Please

....

Gender

☐ ☐ ☐ Rather Not Say

Date of Visit: ·······························

Time of Visit: ·······························

Length of Visit ·······················
(Mins):

During Your Visit, Did You:

☐ Look At Your **Poop**

☐ Browsing Your Phone

☐ *Miss It*

☐ Put Down The Cover

☐ Used More Than Half Roll Of Paper

☐ Wash Your Hand

estimated weight of your 💩 :

☐ .... Grams   ☐ .... Pounds

Your Thoughts and your feelings

....
....
....
....
....
....
....
....
....
....
....
....
....
....
....
....
....
....
....
....
....
....
....
....
....
....
....

Welcome To My Bathroom

 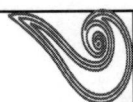

Your Name Please

....

Gender

☐ ☐ ☐ Rather Not Say

Date of Visit: ·······························

Time of Visit: ·····························

Length of Visit ····························
(Mins):

During Your Visit, Did You:

☐ Look At Your **Poop**

☐ Browsing Your Phone

☐ **Miss It**

☐ Put Down The Cover

☐ Used More Than Half Roll Of Paper

☐ **Wash Your Hand**

estimated weight of your 💩 :

[........] Grams   [.......] Pounds

Your Thoughts and your feelings

....
....
....
....
....
....
....
....
....
....
....
....
....
....
....
....
....
....
....
....
....
....
....
....
....
....
....
....
....

 # Welcome To My Bathroom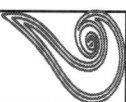

Your Name Please

....

Gender

☐ ☐ ☐ Rather Not Say

Date of Visit: ·····················

Time of Visit: ·····················

Length of Visit ····················
(Mins):

During Your Visit, Did You:

☐ Look At Your **Poop**

☐ Browsing Your Phone

☐ *Miss It*

☐ Put Down The Cover

☐ Used More Than Half Roll Of Paper

☐ Wash Your Hand

estimated weight of your 💩 :

☐......... Grams   ☐....... Pounds

Your Thoughts and your feelings

....
....
....
....
....
....
....
....
....
....
....
....
....
....
....
....
....
....
....
....
....
....
....
....
....
....
....
....
....
....

Welcome To My Bathroom

Your Name Please
....

Gender

☐   ☐   ☐ Rather Not Say

---

estimated weight of your 💩 :

[.........] Grams   [.......] Pounds

Your Thoughts and your feelings

....
....
....
....
....
....
....
....
....
....
....
....
....
....
....
....
....
....
....
....
....
....
....
....
....
....
....
....
....
....
....
....

Date of Visit: ·······························

Time of Visit: ·······························

Length of Visit ····························
(Mins):

During Your Visit, Did You:

☐ Look At Your **Poop**

☐ Browsing Your Phone

☐ *Miss It*

☐ Put Down The Cover

☐ Used More Than Half Roll Of Paper

☐ Wash Your Hand

Welcome To My Bathroom

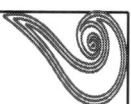

Your Name Please

....

Gender

☐ ☐ ☐ Rather Not Say

Date of Visit: ················

Time of Visit: ················

Length of Visit ················
(Mins):

During Your Visit, Did You:

☐ Look At Your **Poop**

☐ Browsing Your Phone

☐ *Miss It*

☐ Put Down The Cover

☐ Used More Than Half Roll Of Paper

☐ Wash Your Hand

estimated weight of your 💩 :

[..........] Grams   [.......] Pounds

Your Thoughts and your feelings

....
....
....
....
....
....
....
....
....
....
....
....
....
....
....
....
....
....
....
....
....
....
....
....
....

Welcome To My Bathroom

Your Name Please

....

Gender

☐ ☐ ☐ Rather Not Say

Date of Visit: ························

Time of Visit: ························

Length of Visit ·······················
(Mins):

During Your Visit, Did You:

☐ Look At Your *Poop*

☐ Browsing Your Phone

☐ *Miss It*

☐ Put Down The Cover

☐ Used More Than Half Roll Of Paper

☐ *Wash Your Hand*

estimated weight of your  :

┌·········┐ Grams   ┌·······┐ Pounds
└─────────┘   └───────┘

Your Thoughts and your feelings

....
....
....
....
....
....
....
....
....
....
....
....
....
....
....
....
....
....
....
....
....
....
....
....
....
....
....

Made in the USA
Columbia, SC
12 November 2020